ZEN IN THE MARKETS

ZEN IN THE MARKETS

Confessions of a Samurai Trader

Edward Allen Toppel

WARNER BOOKS

A Time Warner Company

Warner Books, Inc., 1271 Avenue of the Americas, New York, N.Y. 10020

 A Time Warner Company

Printed in the United States of America
First Warner Books printing: October 1994
10 9 8 7 6 5 4 3 2 1

Library of Congress Cataloging-in-Publication Data

Toppel, Edward Allen.
    Zen in the markets : confessions of a Samurai trader / Edward
Allen Toppel.
        p. cm.
    Originally published: Chicago : Samurai Press, © 1992.
    Includes bibliographical references.
    ISBN 0-446-51810-7
    1. Floor traders (Finance)—Psychology. 2. Stock-exchange.
3. Zen Buddhism. I. Title.
HG4621.T64 1994
332.64'01'9—dc20   94-298
                                                     CIP

Book design by Giorgetta Bell McRee

This book is dedicated
to those whose warrior souls
have been perfected
and to those of us
who are still trying.

> *Dewdrop, let me rinse*
> *In your swift sweet water*
> *The dark hands of life.*
>
> **BASHO**

The Announcement

Nasrudin stood up in the marketplace and started to address the throng.

"O my people! Do all of you really want knowledge without difficulty, truth without falsehood, great attainment without effort, progress without sacrifice?"

Very soon a very large crowd gathered, everyone shouting, "Yes, yes!"

"Excellent!" said the mullah. "I only wanted to know. You may rely upon me to tell you about it if I ever discover any such a thing."

SUFI TEACHING STORY

Contents

CONTENTS

CONTENTS

Acknowledgments

There are so many people to whom I owe a debt of gratitude that I could fill up this book with their names. Those whom I have forgotten, please forgive me.

Karen; my two wonderful children, Jessica and Neil; my parents, Lilian and Morris; my sister, Gail; and my brother, Lewis.

Harry Brandt, Tom Stone, Jay Zimmerman, Steve Krupnick, Joe Gregory, Bernie Bubman, Roger Nash, Marvin Israel, Craig Anderson, Bert Aronsen, Bruce Frost, William Kennedy, Vic Grossi, Ernie Naiditch, Diane Miller, Constance Trojnar, Susan Holton, Pat Shannon, Larry Belenke, Brigitta Ploessner, Simon Lubershane, Don Cohen, Leo Stein, Jim Scanlon, Bob Jordan, Wayne Selz, Jane Rosenbloom, and Errol Simon.

I thank you for your love and support.

Preface

I have always known
That at last I would
Take this road,
but yesterday I
did not know it would
be today.

NARIHIRA

•

Like Zen, this book is brief and to the point. I have not tried to obscure the simple truths with meaningless pages of charts and statistics. Quality of thought, not quantity of paper is presented here.

The seeds for this book began to take hold after I had a very enlightening experience while trading IBM options during a crazy and hectic day as a market maker at the Chicago Board Options Exchange in 1980.

I didn't realize until I was home what had happened. I had one of my most profitable days ever. Yet I had been totally unaware of myself as I traded. I had virtually lost my self in the trading pit that fateful day.

I began to recall some of the books that I had read on Zen Buddhism in college. I felt that I finally had a taste of what those writers were trying to convey. Thus began my pursuit of this question as it applies to the markets.

Sunnan Kubose of the Buddhist Temple of Chicago comes close to capturing the spirit of Zen when he tries to express a certain aspect of spiritual life. He says, "It is like water gushing from a deep underground spring. Everything is very natural. There is a quality of '*boom!*' because it is done with one's whole life. It is done one hundred percent; life just comes gushing out."

The message of this book is for both the person who glances at the financial pages in the evening to see how his investments are faring and for the full-time professional money manager or floor trader. The ideas of this essay for success in the markets apply to each.

Just remember that you are in a contest with yourself and not the market. This lack of sense of self made the Samurai warrior a powerful and formidable opponent. It takes time, understanding, and hard work to get to this point in any endeavor, especially in trading.

First you must know where you are coming from in order to get to that point of oneness, be it in the markets or anything else that you do. I hope that this book points the way. I know you can do it.

All you have to do is realize what keeps you from being on the right side of the market and resolve to correct that problem. That is where the real work lies.

Good things flow from this realization.

EDWARD ALLEN TOPPEL
Chicago, Illinois
Fall 1994

> *I trade,*
> *therefore I am.*
>
> SAMURAI TRADER'S PHILOSOPHY

ZEN IN THE MARKETS

PART I

Seeing Through Zen Eyes

> *It is too clear and so it is hard to see.*
> *A dunce searched for fire with a lit*
> *lantern. Had he known what fire was*
> *he would have cooked his rice*
> *sooner.*
>
> THE GATELESS GATE

Chapter 1

LOOKS CAN KILL YOU

*I sneezed
and lost sight
of the skylark.*

YAYU

•

The market is an easy game to play. It is just that we are hell-bent upon making it so complicated. That's what makes it so difficult for us to win.

A glance at the dos and don'ts of trading in any market reveals some easily understood and seemingly simple rules to follow. We have all seen them a hundred times. They are the rules that all traders, both professional and nonprofessional, are supposed to follow. Remember, I said *supposed* to follow: the rules have been time and money proven.

The most important and basic rules of trading and investing are as follows:

1. **Buy low, sell high.**
2. **Let profits run, cut losses quickly.**
3. **Add to a winning position, not a loser.**
4. **Go with the trend.**

These rules look simple and are certainly easy to understand. So, how come so many of us kill ourselves in the market? What makes it so difficult to follow these guidelines?

More than likely we've repeatedly broken each of these rules and will probably continue to do so, despite acknowledging that we'll wind up losers if these simple guidelines are not followed. How come? The answer to this question contains the secret for our future success in the market.

The problem lies not within the rules, but within ourselves as we apply these rules to our investments and trading decisions. Yes, the problem is internal, and until we learn to change our perception about what makes the market tick we will continue to punish ourselves and remain on the losing side of the ledger.

This book attempts to offer insight into those teachings that have shaped our responses to the market's very clear directions. Through a retraining of our conditioning and thought processes we can at last begin to see what the market is saying and not what we want it to say. We will be able to hear the market's signals and respond accordingly.

The process of Zen, if it can safely be called a process,

reveals that the market gives clear directions as to what course of action to take. The mental discipline of Zen will help cut through our own fog of self-deception and finally allow us to see clearly and feel the true course of the market. Then we can and will act accordingly.

Zen discipline helps us to dissolve those actions and perceptions that have kept us from the winner's circle. Let's go back to those rules and see what happens to us in spite of knowing the rules.

Instead of buying low, most of us wind up selling low and buying high. The causes are many and the excuses are laughable. "Uncle Joe gave us a hot tip that turned out to be an iceberg. Everybody else was buying Midget Widget, so we jumped in, too. The stock had a good balance sheet. How could it not go up?" All of the wrong reasons, but still very common excuses for getting involved in the market.

We hold on to losing positions and start hoping that the market will turn around and reward us for being a little early in calling the correct direction of a market. That's not the way it works. More than likely we hold on to losers until we can't stand the pressure or have to meet a margin call. Usually we act at the bottom if we are long or at the top if we are short. We're supposed to get out of losers quickly. What kept us from doing this? What makes it so difficult to take our losses? This book answers that question and supplies a simple but difficult solution.

Worse than buying high and selling low is adding to a position that is not already profitable. For example, we bought ABC Bio-Engineering Co. at 22 a share, and it is now selling for 18. Our broker calls and says that the stock is still on their firm's buy list and thinks that we should buy more. The broker tells us to average down our position. We agree and buy another hundred shares. We all know that it is easier to compound our mistakes than to correct them, and that is exactly what happened with that purchase of another hundred shares at a lower price. A losing position was added to, despite our determination not to add to losers.

So, why do we add to losers and punish ourselves and our pocketbooks with this most grievous of investment errors? Why is it easier to add to a mistake than to correct one?

The winning positions are usually cashed in too early. We get a few points of profit and congratulate ourselves for being so smart. Then we watch as the stock or commodity continues to climb, climb, and climb. Why didn't we buy more as the position proved itself a winner? We know the rules, but something inside of us wins over. What is it?

If we can identify this mysterious force, are we willing to contain its power over us?

We have all bought stocks because we thought they were cheap, ones that once sold for 80 and are now selling for 36. Wow, I can now buy it for 36! It's cheap. We can get twice as much, almost like two for the price of one. Sounds crazy, but some of us do it all the time. I can't think of a dumber reason to make an investment decision. The rules say go with the trend. In this case, the trend is certainly down. Yet we fool ourselves into thinking that we are getting bargains.

We're fighting the trend. We can clearly see that the direction is down, yet many of us think nothing of averaging a loser. We know the major rules. What makes us want to break them and place our capital at greater risk?

Every one of the rules that has been tested and proven over time continues to be broken by professional and nonprofessional traders alike. What can we do to insure that these rules are followed to the letter? We can't have a policeman stand over us to make sure we are trading by the rules. So, what can we do?

Enough of the questions. On with the solutions that have worked for those willing to work hard. Notice that word—"work." That's what it takes to correct our errors.

The first step is to recognize the error of our ways and be determined to do something about it. The result will be a permanent change in our behavior as it applies to our attempts to make money in the market. These rules are for stocks, bonds, options or futures, or whatever market you trade. It is all the same. The problem is that we bring to the market a set of notions plus a system of logic that just doesn't work. We must first rid ourselves of these dangerous forms of self-deception before we hear the market's call. Ridding ourselves of ourselves is the most difficult problem we face when attempting to make money in whatever market we're involved.

In reality, the market puts us in a contest with ourselves. Until we let go of the false ideas of what makes the market tick and simply respond as the market unfolds, we will continue to be punished.

The discipline that dissolves the veil of self-deception between you and the market can be attained in many ways. I have found that the spiritual path offered by Zen philosophy and meditation works for me. Through this discipline, we can work at reducing our ego's interference and kiss the old, irrelevant logical systems good-bye.

Rest assured that our egos will fight us every inch of the way. The battle is long and hard. But it is worth every ounce of sweat.

When this is accomplished, we can begin to live and focus in the present moment. The promise of this approach is that once the nature of the beast within is recognized for what it is and we understand the dimensions of its powerful grip on everything we do, we will be able to grasp the flow of the market and be on our way to becoming very successful.

First we must recognize the weapons we are using to sink our financial ship in the murky waters of the market. Once we see that we are our own worst enemy, we will move on to the process of extinguishing such interference from our dealings with the market.

We must first recognize the symptoms before undertaking the cure.

Chapter 2

GETTING RID OF BIG E

Big E. E for error? No, not exactly, but close. Big E is our enemy, the enemy within all of us. Big E is our ego. Let's look at how the ego operates—that is, how it operates us in the market.

We read or hear something and immediately form an opinion, extrapolating the consequences of the information that we have just consumed. If we are wise, we will see whether the market confirms our opinion. More than likely we'll just jump in and take our position no matter what the market is saying. Then we wait for the market to prove us right. Sometimes it agrees with us immediately, and our position becomes an instant winner.

When it doesn't, the trouble begins. Ego starts to tighten its grip over our ability to do the right thing. The right thing is to get rid of our losers immediately. The ego will produce the most fantastic reasons for holding on to that money-draining position, be it in stocks, bonds, options, or futures. Ego will fight us all the way and prevent us from realizing quickly that it is better to swallow our pride and do the right thing. Take the loss before it becomes expensive. We know the rule that says take those losses quickly and move on. Ego gets between us and the rules in order to preserve its self-esteem. Really, ego has a life of its own within all of us. Its hold is more powerful than a plutonium bomb.

When I was a broker with Bear, Stearns & Co., some of my clients would say that they didn't have a loss until they took it. They would hang on until the market proved that they were right. How ridiculous and how very expensive it was for some of them. Again, ego imposes its will over what we know to be the correct action. Objectivity tells us we are wrong. Ego tells us to hang on.

When we have a winner, ego manifests itself by coaxing us into taking our profits quickly. Why didn't it get us out of our losses quickly? The ego will get us out of our winners fast because it needs the immediate gratification of being right. It likes being right. It will deny being wrong. Fire our ego? Hard to do. Being aware of our ego's tight grip is a start.

You can reduce ego's hold in your investment practices through very hard work. Playing the market is the hardest way to make an easy living. Egos won't die.

Just being aware of the power of this force gets you started in the right direction.

Egoless people have nothing to protect. They just do whatever the market tells them to do. They don't tell the market what to do or what it is going to do. They have no ego directing them, so it is very easy to flow with the market's directions. What's difficult is ridding ourselves of our ego. It takes a lot of training, years and years of it for some of us. It's like school. When you pay attention to what the teacher says, you get good grades. In this case the market is our teacher, and it pays to listen.

The Zen approach is to realize the many dangers of an ego-led trading and investment style and determine not to be misled by our ego. Easier said than done, but it is not impossible. People have been known to meditate for years before being able to unshackle themselves from the tight grip of their ego. Some fortunate ones have a natural ability to act in an egoless fashion. They are easily identified, for they are the big winners in the market. Other parts of their lives are affected positively as well.

For us to become egoless, and therefore more likely to succeed where we have failed previously, requires a new way of viewing the market. Egoless sight is seeing things for what they are and not for what our ego would like them to be. No distortions change what's in front of our eyes. We act upon what we see, not what we want to see.

There is simply no hoping, no praying, and no weird rationalizing. The truth revealed without ego's interference is our goal.

What Zen shows us is that we are truly one with the market. The market isn't here and we are there. We don't have to beat the market. The market will give us what we earn. Just open up those egoless eyes and listen to what the market wants to tell us, not what we want to tell the market.

What I am saying is that the market makes all the decisions. Our only decision is to listen, feel, and respond to the market's siren. Always and without exception. Remember, the market never lies. It is only we who lie to ourselves.

Chapter 3

SAYING GOOD-BYE TO ARISTOTLE

Most of us come to the market with the notion that if certain events happen, the market should react in this or that way. The market will go up or down because of this event. Let us call this Aristotelian logic, and let us promptly recognize that Aristotle belongs in universities and not in markets.

Examine certain major events in the world and their effect on the markets. It's the summer of 1982, and Mexico has announced that it can't make payments on the $100 billion that it owes. A default of that magnitude should have quaked the market in a big way. What really happened was the beginning of the biggest bull market in history. The Dow was in the 700s. Ten years later, the averages have nearly quadrupled. Figure that one out, Aristotle!

Each and every day the savings and loan disaster gets larger. It is going to cost the government much more than $500 billion to shore up that mess. Each day the figure gets larger, and the market yawns as though it's a non-event. Perhaps the market knows that you and I are going to wind up paying for it. Where's the $500 billion going to come from, anyway? Why hasn't the market reacted to this news? Didn't we read in Economics 101 that such a huge dent in the taxpayer's pocketbook is bearish for the market? The market is telling us not to worry. It's saying, "Forget what we were taught in school. It doesn't fit the scheme of things here. None of that schoolbook logic applies here."

The Japanese stock market tumbled nearly 30 percent in the first quarter of 1990. "How bearish for world markets," is what the logicians said. They were right for only one world market, the Japanese stock market. Nearly every other world market went higher and did not fall. Those who said there would be a delayed reaction were only covering for their ego's failed predictions. We are concerned about what is happening here and now, not what might or might not occur in the future. In the business of the market, the here and now is all that there is. The future is now, the past is forgotten, and we focus on the present moment. Logic only gets in the way.

Balance sheets and P/E ratios are only one small part of the picture. *How well you play the inner game is what determines whether you will be successful making money in the markets.*

We must realize that the market defies logic. It has a logic all its own, and it won't tell us in advance what its reaction to events will be. We can watch for clues and then react. Basically the best we can hope for is quick reaction time to the market's signals. We must first wait and then follow, not interpret. When we interpret correctly, we claim omniscience. What we get is a false sense of empowerment. When we are wrong, we forget about our miscalculations. How insidiously clever is the ego.

The dartboard throwers have proven that they are much better than most money managers. The rush to indexing, a popular form of investing, is an admission that the managers can't figure out the direction of the market either! Megabillions have been put into index funds. All these funds want to do is be average. They are willing to settle for being average because their managers know that the market can't be figured out. They know that if they try, they'll probably wind up below average. Indexing is a sure way to be safe and to get paid. They do neither better nor worse than the averages.

If the market were logical, we'd all be winners. So let's give up applying a system of expected outcomes to that phenomenon that has eluded the best minds sifting through a multitude of data for their analyses.

Even the carefully programmed computers can't give reliable information. The brightest minds in the world can't figure it out, so how can we expect to do it? Our old nemesis ego will tell us that it has and will provide enough of the ammunition to support its false conclusions.

It is very difficult for the mind to just watch the market unfold. Our minds, egos, left hemispheres, must get into the act no matter now many times they have been proven to be painfully incapable of doing the job consistently.

Just give up the idea that we can figure it out! Listen to the market shout a very clear and unmistakable direction to us. All we have to do is listen, feel, and follow the market's signals and not hope the market follows our lead. Rest assured. It won't!

Chapter 4

HANGING OUT IN THE PRESENT

Who cares about what happened yesterday? The markets are like the dice in a crap game. They have no memory. Only we do. What happened in the past has no known effect upon the market. But our memories are strong. We would like to think that history matters. Then we can worry and speculate about the effects of yesterday's events upon today's market.

The stock market crash of October 1987 signaled to many the end of the bull market. They looked back to the events following the crash of 1929 and clearly saw how the future would unfold. Wrong! Instead the market steadily gained strength and continued on its merry way. Those who kept thinking about the past couldn't believe their eyes.

If they thought that there were parallels between the crash

of 1929 and the crash of 1987 and that the market would follow a similar pattern, they were badly punished. If they played the short side of the market, they were severely punished. Every moment is unique, and every market is very different. Predictions about the future based upon similarities to the past are worthless.

Had we kept our eyes on the present moment instead of focusing on the past, waiting for the stock market to sink once again, we would have ridden the market back to the new highs that it saw in the first half of 1994. Those who said that they couldn't believe the market could recover from such a severe blow and go on to post new historical highs missed yet another great opportunity. Believe what you see, not what you think. If seeing is believing, then we have to learn to accept what we see.

The historians raked over the dying embers of the Japanese stock market when it dropped more than 30 percent in early 1990. Many have noted that following past crashes in the Japanese markets, it has taken five to six years for prices to recover to the level of share prices prior to the crash. No one thought that the U.S. stock market would recover and set new highs so quickly. What makes them think that the Japanese market couldn't do the same? Focus on the present moment and you will not be fooled by any historical nonsense.

Many traders and investors rely on charts to make their trading and investment timing decisions. Those little *x*s and *o*s that the chartist uses are nothing but a record of yesterday's events. They have absolutely no predictive value.

All they show is that there may or may not be support or resistance at a given price level. No kidding.

A chartist will say that a market has broken out if it goes through a certain area of resistance. They will also say that a market has broken down if it goes through a support area. Charts are total gibberish. They have no validity. They are simply history, and like history, if we continue to study them, we will probably commit the same errors of the past.

History doesn't repeat itself. Neither in the stock market nor anywhere else.

We must keep our focus in the here and now. Charts, economic analyses, news articles, and investment reports distract us from focusing on the present moment. At best all we can do is reflect the market. If the market is the sun, let us be the shadow. We shouldn't attempt to predict future direction. All we have to do is follow the clear and easily recognized signals that are given.

Remember, all we have to do is stay in the present moment. Don't think about the past or the future. Focus on the here and now, and listen to the voice of the market.

The remainder of the book presents the Zen approach to successful trading and reveals how to listen, recognize, and obey the language that every market speaks.

We do not see things as they are
but as we are.

Samurai Trader's Maxim Number One

> *To find your self,*
> *you must lose your self first.*

PART II

Zen Sins

> *You can break the rules and get away with it. Eventually, the rules break you for not respecting them.*
>
> THE SHEP'S TRADING RULE

Chapter 5

DOUBLE UP TO BELLY UP

*If the white herons
had no voice
they would be lost
in the morning snow.*

CHIYO

•

Far and away the worst error anyone can commit is to add
to a position that is a loser. There is no worse curse than
making money while violating this most cardinal of trading rules. We are only setting ourselves up for the one that
doesn't come back. Averaging, as it is called, means that we
are going against the grain of the market. Our initial decision was wrong, and now it is compounded by our hoping
that the market won't have to come back much in order to
show a profit.

For example, we initially purchased XYZ at 20 and now it is selling at 16, and we decide to buy more. We would be guilty of adding to a losing position. The converse is true for the short side. We are hoping that the trend of the market will reverse soon in order to prove our initial decision right. Often it does. When it doesn't, major hemorrhaging occurs.

Doubling up is predicated on the hope that the market will reverse itself. It flies in the face of the trend at that moment. Who says that a market has to reverse itself? For a real chuckle, go through *Barron's* and see how many pundits thought the stock market couldn't go any higher. They cited all sorts of statistics based on past markets. Start in 1985 when the Dow was just in the 1200s. Each and every month another market guru came along, arguing that the market couldn't go any higher. If you had listened to them and played the short side, you would have only had to wait until 1994 for the Dow to maybe peak out. If you had been doubling up on the short side every 100 Dow points, you would have gone very, very broke.

When that one-day crash on October 19, 1987, finally happened, you would have been committing financial suicide had you been a buyer averaging your losers.

Because something once sold for 80 and now sells for 40 doesn't make it cheap or a bargain. When I was a young broker I heard people say that a stock was a bargain because it had dropped so much and nothing had changed in the company. The Shadow knows, and so does the market. I had a customer who started buying Penn Central when the stock sold in the 70s. He bought more as the stock's price dropped to single digits. Even though I warned him about the rule of not adding to a bad position, he continued to buy more shares. Eventually Penn Central went broke. My client didn't go broke, but he took a hit in the millions! Who knows where a stock will stop when it's going up or down?

Doubling up has ruined a lot of people. In order to double up, you must go against the flow. You are saying, "I know that the market is going to turn and prove me right." No one knows when or how! The market is like the little ball in a roulette wheel. It goes round and round, and no one knows where it will stop. We can go along for the ride, though.

We double up because our egos do not like being wrong. They tell us to hold on, gut it out, double up, do anything but admit that we are wrong. Our ego will invent the weirdest rationalizations for adding to the losing position. It will go through strange mathematical constructions showing that because our average cost is lower, we can get out profitably with just a slight reversal in the trend. But who can tell when that reversal will come? Certainly not the writers in *Barron's* and other leading financial journals or the scores of bearish investment letter writers who persisted on calling an end to the bull market.

I know of one trader who doubled up and got away with it for years until the great crash of 1987. In one day, the market took back everything he had made during those years he had been doubling up and making money. It is like Russian roulette. Eventually you are going to buy the bullet if you keep pulling the trigger long enough. That's just the way it works.

Our egos trick us into doubling up a losing position. They refuse to look directly at reality. They want to be right no matter what the cost. A lot of people would rather be right than make money. Their egos are making all the decisions.

Doubling up works more times than it doesn't. Unfortunately, we never know when it won't. Always remember that the day we try it could be the start of another October 19, 1987. When we double up, we eventually go belly up!

Chapter 6

SMALL IS BIG, BIG IS SMALL

How big a position you should take in the market usually is governed by the amount of money in your account. It seems that when you trade a small number, things go right. No matter what you do, you are a winner. Money rolls in. Your account swells.

Many people are not content to have their accounts roll up the dough. They will always want to accelerate the process of money accumulation. They reason that if they traded a certain size, all they have to do is increase that number, and they will increase their earning power.

Somehow, it just doesn't work that way. When we increase the size of our positions, a funny thing happens. We usually begin to lose money. And a lot of it. It all depends on how you increase your size. Weight lifters gradually put more iron on the bar. They don't suddenly go from one hundred to three hundred pounds. They go in small increments. Our minds are very much like muscles. They can handle only a gradual increase in the risk that we assume in the market. Too sudden a shift in risk size disturbs our equilibrium and sense of the market's ebbs and flows.

I'll give you an example. I know traders who are consistent winners. They trade a small size. In the S&P pit at the Chicago Mercantile Exchange, where I trade, there are traders who never trade bigger than a one lot. When they do, they invariably lose. They have found a number that their minds can accept. Some have gradually increased their number and been successful. Others have tried to jump from one to ten and were eventually destroyed. The market is like Santa Claus: it knows when we've been bad.

Eventually we reach a number that we can't seem to exceed. We can be successful at one level but not at a higher one. I guess there is a Peter Principle in trading, too. We all reach our level of incompetency. It seems the smaller numbers always work. Gradual increases in risk seem to work also.

Most of the big traders I have known eventually met their own Waterloo. Some are truly great and continue to trade huge numbers. Most, however, must return to being small traders. It has happened to me many times. The pain of losing lots of hard-earned cash eventually returns the ego to its proper proportion. Why is it that this phenomenon of size occurs? What makes it difficult to trade large numbers and continue to be successful? What magical power takes over when we've increased our risk and sense of adventure?

Knowing that this law of size increase results in a disaster, why can't we restrain ourselves and live with this truth? What keeps us returning to retest this great law? Our egos' insistence that this won't happen again seems to overpower our judgment. It can't believe that it isn't ready to be a bigger trader.

Our sense of self is enhanced by size, be it in trading large numbers, living in a big house, driving a big car, or owning a big boat. Our egos swell in proportion to the bigness of our risk assumption. Egos want to be bloated, and one way is to trade bigger than we are capable of doing successfully.

Egos often will deny the reality of their inability to function at a higher risk level. They will tell us that they have it under control this time and that they are strong enough to do well at a greater trading size.

The pain of being wrong seems to increase exponentially in relation to the size of the position. If we normally trade one lots and now we are trading twos, the degree of difficulty in acting quickly when we are wrong is not twice but perhaps five times as great. Herein lies the magic that seems to cast its spell on each trader's psyche. The pain to our ego is in proportion to the size of trades. Avoidance of pain is what keeps us from acting fast. Losing that fear is the key to success. We must trust the process.

Very few people have problems taking profits. The ability to take losses quickly is what separates the great market players from the also-rans. It is also what separates us from our money. This ability is a function of the ego's willingness to admit that it is wrong. The person with the smallest ego can take losses quickly. Also, the smaller position usually results in a smaller loss. The smaller the amount of pain the ego has to work through, the less time it will take to get it out of the way.

There is a paralysis that sets in when the losses begin to mount. These losses are much too much for the ego to admit. It would rather deny and postpone judgment day than face the truth.

The greater the size, the greater the pain when we are on the wrong side of the flow of the market. It's easier to swallow our medicine when the pills are small than when they are big.

Chapter 7

PADDLING IN THE RIVER

Buy high, sell higher. Sell low, buy lower. That's the way the old saw about making money in the market should read.

To do otherwise is to be guilty of picking tops or bottoms. Both are deadly ego games. When a market is moving in one direction, it is more likely than not to continue to move in that direction. To get in its way is to swim against the river. Usually when we swim against the current, we get very tired and don't go too far. Sometimes we drown.

That's the way it is in the market, too. He who fights the current of the marketplace doesn't get very far. Sure, we've heard about contrarians who made money fading the crowd. In reality they made money only when the market changed direction. What happens when it doesn't change or it takes years before a turnaround? They've wasted a lot of time and money. The situation here is the same as that with wine: there's no need to take a position until it is time. So, when is that time? How do we know when it is time to buy or sell? Perfect timing is impossible. If we try to buy or sell against the trend, we are relying too much on luck.

Luck runs out eventually. Anyone who gets into a position too early is crystal-ball gazing. It is better to get on the train as it is leaving the station than to get in front of it as the train appears to be coming to the end of the line. This could just be the end of the line for us.

Buying into a downtrending market is presumptuous. We assume that we know where the turn is. We are more likely to win the lottery than to be able to pick a turn. Ego likes to play this game. When I read or hear people claiming they bought the bottom or sold the top or have a system that does it, I say a prayer for them. They have obviously been very lucky. I hope that they know it. Top picking is the flip side of bottom fishing. We are fighting the river. We may win once in a while, and that's bad because it bloats our ego and gives it a false sense of omniscience. The river always wins. Paddle with the stream.

The greatest warrior is one who
conquers himself.

Samurai Trader's Maxim Number Two

When I eat, I eat.

When I walk, I walk.

When I sleep, I sleep.

ZEN SAYING

PART III

Making Zense of the Markets

> We must learn to differentiate clearly
> the fundamentally important, that
> which is really basic, from that which
> is dispensable, and to turn aside from
> everything else, from the multitude of
> things which clutter up the mind and
> divert it from the essential.
>
> ALBERT EINSTEIN

Chapter 8

ZEN VISION AND I.Q. TEST

The cuckoo calls
and suddenly...
the bamboo grove
lighted by moonbeams

BASHO

•

To see things as they are and not the way you want them to be requires good vision and a reasonable intellect. Actually, it is better if we have no intellect working at all. This test will illustrate what it takes to be a success using a Zen approach to the market.

Start with the vision test. Keep this page at a reasonable distance from your nose. Now read aloud the following numbers:

27   28   29

Did you say twenty-seven, twenty-eight, and twenty-nine? Brilliant! You've passed the second-hardest part of doing well in the market.

Now for the hardest part. Look again at the numbers and say out loud the number that is the highest. Now say the lowest. Which number is between both numbers?

Did you say that twenty-seven was the lowest and that twenty-nine was the highest? If you also said that twenty-eight was in the middle, then you've passed the test with flying colors! You are on your way to being very successful in the markets. You may be laughing, but I am dead serious. If it really is that simple to recognize what the market is saying at all times, why do you have to complicate it?

The vision test that you have taken proves that you can recognize different numbers, and the I.Q. test demonstrates that you know the relationships among them. Believe me when I say that no other knowledge of the market is necessary.

This exam determines that you are clearly capable of an egoless view of the market—a Zen view, if you wish. A view that is free of personality needs. Twenty-nine is higher than twenty-seven. No one can dispute that. Not even your ego, no matter how hard it may try.

You've proven beyond a shadow of a doubt that you can tell when you've got a profit and when you've got a loss. There is no question about it. Absolutely none.

When you buy something at 27 and it goes to 29, you know that you are showing a profit. Absolutely no doubt about it. Conversely, when you do the opposite, you know that you are sitting with a loser.

If you bought at 29 and now the price is lower, you must recognize that you have a loss. Don't rationalize and say that you don't have a loss until you sell. And don't say that you know it will come back. You don't know that, either.

And if you say it's a long-term investment, you're just kidding yourself. That's just another way of not having to deal with a mistake. Your ego is just hoping, trying to shield itself from the pain of being wrong. You've proven that you know the difference between a profit and a loss. That's the easy part. Doing something about it is where the difficulty lies.

Before going farther, let's review once more the basic rules all successful investors and traders must constantly follow in order to profit in the market.

These rules are as follows:

1. **Never add to a loser.**
2. **Add to a winner only.**
3. **Let profits run.**
4. **Cut losses fast.**
5. **Don't pick tops.**
6. **Don't pick bottoms.**

And most important of all:

7. **Let the market make the decisions, not your ego.**

The rules are not hard to understand. Recognizing a profit from a loss is simple. If the rules are easy to grasp and a profit is distinguishable from a loss, where does the problem lie? What makes it so hard to apply the rules?

There is something within each of us that has a power over our minds that prevents our acting according to what we have agreed is the proper course of action. That something is present in all of us and is very powerful, more powerful than anything I know. Let's call it ego. Until we learn to get rid of our ego, we will never make money in the market consistently. Those who haven't identified the ego's ways will eventually be destroyed in the market because of their ego's tendencies. It is just that powerful. The market rewards those who have subdued their egos.

Those who rid themselves of their egos are rewarded greatly. They are the superstars of their fields. In the market, rewards come in the form of profits. In the world of art, masterpieces are the results. In sports, the players are all-stars and command enormous salaries. Every pursuit has its own manifestation of victory over the ego.

Chapter 9

LISTENING TO THE MASTER

Do yourself a favor. Do not read this chapter until you have read all of the previous chapters. It won't make a lot of sense to you. You'll be wasting a lot of time. It takes a while for the message to sink in and have meaning for you.

The perfect master? It is always right and never lies; tells you what to do, when to do it, when it changes its mind; and speaks lucidly in a language you can quickly understand. Listen to the master, and you will never be sorry. You will be rewarded greatly. You have to pay a price, however.

The perfect master is the market itself. The market speaks to us in one language—price. Numbers, if you will. Numbers that you can recognize and differentiate. You proved that in a previous chapter. More than likely you have been listening to a different sound. That noise is your ego's voice. Stop listening and turn to the only expert worth following—the market. Don't make it difficult and obscure this simple truth. Forget your voice, and listen to the clear message and direct call given off by the market. Just feel, follow, and put full faith in your ability to blend with the leader, not attempt to lead the market. Now let us see how to apply the market's directions to our own actions.

As long as a market is rising, it is safe to buy into it. You are going with the flow. A liquid market is a lot easier to get out of and reverse. A thin market is dangerous.

How do you know if a market is rising? Simple! Look at the last sale. Is it higher or lower than the previous sale? If it is higher, it must be going up. Yes, it may go down again, but we do not know that. Remember, all we are concerned about is what is happening in the present moment. That's all that counts. Stay in the present moment. That's all there is for sure. All other thoughts are pure speculation by the ego. Does anyone know the future? How can your ego tell what the next moment will bring? Right now your ego is probably telling you it can't be this simple, but it is. Tell your ego to take a hike!

Staying in the present moment takes great concentration. Whatever the trend is, you must assume that it will continue. You will know when it reverses because the prices will change. A market jiggles back and forth, producing many momentary price changes in each direction. Only a very strong person will be able to play each switch. This is exhausting, and I know of no one who can be switching back and forth constantly. If you are an investor who is not on top of the market every second, you simply have to devise some kind of switch parameter that allows you to monitor the market and your positions. Perhaps it is a standing stop-loss order based on percentage of capital at risk. There is no hard-and-fast rule here.

If the market moves in a narrow range, there can be a lot of switching before a major move occurs. We call this being chopped. Remember, it is far better to be chopped for a while than to be beaten completely. Eventually that will be the case if we continue to hold a loser too long.

Usually people will add to a loser more easily than to a winner. There is an urge to deny our mistakes by adding to losers. When individuals hold losers, they usually begin to rationalize their error by saying that they are long-term investors. If they had a quick profit, they probably would have taken it. Brokers often tell their customers not to look at the short term, especially when their recommendation turns out to be a clinker. That's a cheap way of not being accountable *now* for losing their clients' money. It is a form of deceit.

Adding to winners is simply trending. As long as the position continues in the right direction, we should add. The right side of the market is easily defined. The direction is defined as higher and higher prices if we are long and lower and lower if we are short.

Think about the bull market of the eighties. All you had to do was to buy and buy and buy as prices went higher and higher and higher. Those who thought that they could pick a top were punished severely, including me. Investors or traders who put their trust in these principles were rewarded beyond their wildest expectations.

A market can change direction quickly. It is emotionally and physically exhausting to keep up with each swing. The best we can do is stay in the present moment and see what the next moment brings.

Each trader or investor must define what he thinks a moment is. For a floor trader, it can be the smallest change in direction. For an armchair investor, it can be looked at from closing price to closing price. Some mathematicians think that they can provide a switch parameter based upon historical price movements and statistical formulas. Beware of these people and their systems!

Stay in the moment and don't let the ego take over. Give yourself an ego check to see if your ego has taken over. Simply ask yourself if you are holding on to a losing position. If you are, you have all the evidence you need to know that your ego has taken over. *Take back control, immediately, by getting out of that position.*

It is this simple, yet it is hard to do. Believe it, and just do it!

Chapter 10

NO TICKEE, NO TRADEE

Ticks are the last sale as reported in the market. They are the true language of the market as far as the Zen-oriented trader is concerned. Ticks don't lie. They tell us when we are right and when we are wrong. They tell us when it is time to get in and when to get out. Last sale is what determines your equity at that point. The last sale is truth.

Reading the last price report is an easy function. Understanding what it means is not too difficult either. The herculean task is to respond to its message without hesitation. If it says time to get in, get in. When the last sale indicates time to get out, get out. You know when you have a winner, and you know when you have a loser. What you do about it is what makes the difference between those who are merely lucky and those who have overcome their egos.

Everybody knows someone who made a lot of money in

the market, only to blow it later. They were just lucky. Many people come and go in the market because it is against human nature to adhere to the rules all of the time. They require inhuman self-control. I know of so very few arenas where so much concentration is required and so much is at stake. It really is like being engaged in hand-to-hand combat. Instead of your life, it is your money that's on the line.

Some people are smart enough to know they don't have it and stay away from the market. Others play the market and find out the hard way what's required. If they have the fortitude and willingness to learn from their mistakes, they might make it. Luck can carry you only so far. Eventually the market weeds out those who rely on luck to survive.

Floor traders bum out rapidly because of the high degree of concentration required. Also, the markets are very unforgiving. You can't let your ego dominate your trading. Not ever. Most traders slip in and out of an ego-dominated trading style. They are hot when their ego isn't present and cold when it returns.

If you begin to believe what you have read in these past nine chapters, you are on your way to understanding what is really required for success in the market. Years of hard work are needed just to let go of our egos. Or, is it for our egos to let go of us?

Let the market tell you what to do.

The ideal action
is one that leaves
not a split second
between the urge to action
and the action itself.

Samurai Trader's Maxim Number Three

> *If you find a path with no obstacles,*
> *it probably doesn't lead anywhere.*
>
> THOUGHTS OF REV. SUNNAN KUBOSE

PART IV

Zen Diagnosis, Prescription, and Confession

> *How long the road is but for all the time the journey has already taken. How you have needed every second of it in order to know what the road passes by.*
>
> DAG HAMMARSKJÖLD

Chapter 11

EGOITIS AND ITS TREATMENT

The moon rises.
Leaf upon leaf
flutters down.

SHI KI

•

By now you must know that the enemy of all traders/investors is their egos. I call this powerful grip that ego has on us *egoitis*. I've coined the word to describe the fear our egos have of losing their relevancy in our decision-making processes.

Your ego will fight you and probably win in more ways than you can imagine. You'll know the right thing to do, whether it is getting out of losers or adding to winners, yet you won't be able to act. Often you will do the opposite of what you perceive is the right course of action. Such is the really unbelievable power our enemy within has over our behavior.

Half the battle is recognizing the grip ego can hold on us. It is truly hypnotic at times. The other half is undoing its powerful grip.

One of the cruelest ways ego can affect our profit potential is to help us cut our profits short. The rules say that we should let our profits run and cut our losses short. Most of us find that we do just the opposite. What happens is that our egos want to show off their brilliance by seeking profits. The ego is like a little child. It wants instant gratification. Taking profits early gives that quick reward.

Ego will avoid the pain associated with losing. Strange messages are sent to your brain on behalf of the ego's position. These little memos from your ego will encourage you to take profits quickly, double up on a bad position, let your losses run, and trade bigger than you should.

If you double up on a losing position, the message will be that it will only take a smaller reversal in the market's direction to get you on the profit side. For sure your ego will not tell you that maybe the market won't reverse its direction for a long, long time. It is very good at hiding the truth.

Egoitis is a relative term. People are afflicted in varying degrees. Those showing minor doses of egoitis find they can see the market much clearer than those who are affected by a crippling amount of this human affliction. The market always punishes those people who lead the market with their ego-derived trading strategies. You simply can't see through your own fog of self-deception when the ego decides what the future will bring. It slows the reaction time.

The ego generates opinions based on its own needs. You can't get a clear picture of what's happening in the market if your mind is already made up. You have to trade with an empty mind.

Those who let their egos dominate their behavior are eventually punished. For sure, they are humbled in the long run, as the market requires obedience and will mete out its punishment to all those who won't listen.

Really lucky persons will realize that they have been lucky and quit before the market catches up with them. Very few do until it is too late. Those who have learned to suppress their egos will stand a much greater chance of survival. The person who has really mastered his ego's quirks will thrive. In the trading business we call it discipline.

If the ego is the enemy that I have described, then how do you reduce its influence? Wouldn't it be great if the bio-engineers could find the gene that houses the ego? They could just remove it and replace it with the discipline gene. Somehow I don't think that they ever will. So, what are we mere mortals to do?

A Zen approach would be to simply sit on it. Sit on what? Not your ego, although that is what eventually happens. I'm talking about getting rid of your ego through the process of meditating.

Zazen, as this form of meditation is known in the world of Zen, requires the meditator to sit quietly in a prescribed position and still his mind. Many a novice meditator is asked simply to count his breaths and watch any thoughts come and go through his mind. It is difficult to still the mind completely. For the tyro it is even harder. Like everything else, practice makes perfect.

The benefit of this practice is a reduction in the role ego plays in the decision-making process. In trading this can be most beneficial. Be assured that any attempt to rid one's self of the ego is a monumental task. Zen monks sit for years in order to get a glimpse at enlightenment.

Many people take up the martial arts as a supplement to their Zazen practice. One can never fully get rid of the ego's powerful influence. At best a person can continue to reduce its control over his perception of the world.

Many books are written on the subject of getting rid of one's ego. I prefer the rigor of Zazen. It works for me when I devote the time and discipline necessary to deepen my practice. It is not for everybody. Some people turn to yoga, chanting, painting, transcendental meditation, Open Focus® training, or any other discipline that works to reduce ego's power over us and help us stay in the flow.

If it gets rid of the ego's powerful influence, that is all that matters. At best a person can continue to reduce its control. There are lots of books out there that give advice on how to meditate. Many major cities have Zen centers that offer meditation instruction to the would-be novice. These centers usually offer other disciplines that would supplement your meditation practice. In the suggested readings section at the back of this book I have listed one book on meditation that I have found to be inspiring as well as poetic. I am sure there are a number of others.

Group meditating seems to work for many. The association with other meditators seems to strengthen the resolve to get into the flow and not oppose it. Meditating requires a faith that your ego will fight. You can't explain why it works. You just have to see the results in your life to know that it is very powerful. It takes a higher power to fight the power of one's ego.

For market participants, this means not basing decisions on ego's needs. You cannot really appreciate the power of your ego until you begin to trade. At this point you know in your head what I am talking about in this realm. A lot of people come to the market saying they have control over their ego, only to discover sadly how powerful a force it really is over them.

Your ability to go with the flow is directly proportional to the degree that you are operated by your ego. The more dominated you are by your ego, the more unlikely it is that you will be able to hear, feel, and respond to the market's clear signals.

It is simply the *willingness* to let go of your ego and let the market guide you in your actions that will make the difference in your being a winner. One of the surest and hardest ways to help you conquer your ego is to meditate. It is not easy. Stay with it. You'll be amazed at the results. Don't be spooked. This is powerful medicine.

Obviously, this is just one person's prescription. Experiment and see what works for you. Only then will you find out what the market really represents.

Author's Note: This book mentions the word *ego* many times. It cannot be stressed enough how hard your ego will fight to survive every attempt to lessen its influence in your actions and decision-making processes. Making you painfully aware of its dimensions and strength is no easy task. Perhaps the repetitiveness of this chapter may help.

Chapter 12

MY CONFESSION

Have you ever heard the saying "Do as I say, not as I do"? We all know how much easier it is to tell the next guy what to do than it is to do it ourselves. If I told you that I never break any of these rules and that I meditate every day for at least an hour, I would be lying. I don't, and I don't know anyone who can. Some come close.

My own pattern is to trade without my ego for months on end. After piling up a lot of money, a funny thing happens. My ego creeps back into my trading. As days go by, I fall back into those old ego traps. I don't meditate as frequently as I should. I stop exercising and visualizing. Guess what also happens? I begin to lose a lot of money.

Truthfully, my trading career has been a wild rollercoaster ride. I've always been long on enthusiasm and short on discipline. It takes a tremendous amount of personal discipline to do well trading. That goes for floor traders and off-floor traders as well. Very few people can muster that kind of discipline on a nonstop, everyday basis. I can't, but I do know a few people who can. They are the supertraders, and they deserve the rewards. We all admire their discipline and wish we had more of it. I'm getting better at it, but I still have a long way to go. Maybe by the time I'm ninety I'll have it down. One of the wealthiest traders I know told me it took him twenty years to get it right, and he was a fast learner.

Sometimes I feel that my trading pattern is like that of a stunt flyer. I try to dive as low as possible. Just before I am about to crash, I pull back on the stick and ascend to new heights. Several times the belly of my plane has scraped the ground. On my next climb, I'm going to find a comfortable cloud and retire.

To be a superior trader is to be a warrior. A warrior never lets up on his discipline. He is prepared for the next encounter. A famous Samurai battle cry was *"Katte, kabuto no o o shime yo."* Translated it means, "After victory, tighten your helmet cords." It is very appropriate for anyone involved in the markets. You may have won this battle. Be prepared for the next and the next and the next. The battle with your ego is never ending. Never forget that.

I can tell you what to do as a trader, but until you actually start trading, you will not fully understand, nor will you be able to fully develop a trust that allows you to go with your gut feeling. That is essential for success. Many traders seem to feel the moves as they are occurring. They trust these feelings and go with them. They are truly one with the market. When they are wrong they have the ability to correct their mistakes quickly. These are the real Samurai traders.

Perhaps the following parable will help you understand what I mean about the value of experience.

The Art of Burglary

The son of a burglar saw his father growing older and thought, If he is unable to carry out his profession, who will be the breadwinner of this family, except me? I must learn the trade. He told his father, who approved of his conclusion. One night the father took the son to a big house, broke through the wall, entered the house, and, after opening a large chest, told his son to get in and pick out some clothing. As soon as the son got into the chest, the lid was dropped and the lock securely applied. The father now came out to the courtyard and, knocking loudly at the door, woke up the whole family, whereafter he slipped through the hole in the wall.

The residents got excited and lit candles but found that the burglars had already gone. The son remained all the time in the chest securely confined, thinking of his cruel father. He was mortified.

Suddenly a great idea flashed to him. He made a sound like the gnawing of a rat. The family told the maid to take a candle and examine the chest. When the lid was unlocked, out came the prisoner, who blew out the light and then pushed away the maid and fled.

The people ran after him. Noticing a well by the road, he picked up a large stone and threw it into the water. His pursuers gathered around the well, trying to find the burglar drowning in the dark hole.

In the meantime, he was safely back in his father's house. He blamed the latter very much for his narrow escape. Said the father, "Be not offended, my son. Just tell me how you got off." When the son told him all about his adventures, the father remarked, "There you are, you have learned the art of burglary."

Good luck through good meditating.

> **Expect nothing,
> be prepared for everything.**
>
> *Samurai Trader's Maxim Number Four*

> *Pessimism never won any battles.*
>
> THOUGHTS OF REV. SUNNAN KUBOSE

PART V

Zen Tools for Traders

Focus on your purpose.

SAMURAI TRADER'S MAXIM NUMBER FIVE

Chapter 13

INNER GAME TECHNIQUES

.

The old pond
A frog jumps in
Plop.

BASHO

•

Before I start trading each day I do some mental training. I like to call it inner-game trading techniques. Usually I do these at home before I leave for the exchange. The order in which I do them is important, as each step is built upon the state of mind produced by the previous technique.

In this book I mentioned the importance of meditating in order to clear the mind of distractions. There are numerous styles of meditating. You should investigate as many of them as possible and choose the one that works best for you. None of them is inherently better than any other. It really is a matter of investigation and experimentation to see which style fits you best.

STEP ONE: MEDITATION

I try to meditate at least twenty minutes a day, usually shortly after I awaken. Sometimes I even meditate at night, depending upon how discombobulated I am from a hectic day. Here is what I do. I have a meditation cushion in my bedroom. I simply sit down, slowly fold my long legs, and nearly close my eyes while maintaining a posture that keeps my back fairly erect. Next, I breathe slowly and deeply until I feel relaxed. When thoughts enter my mind, and they do, I do not engage them but simply watch them go to and fro. Eventually they stop.

After all thoughts have ceased to arise in my mind, I just sit and do not focus on anything. I try to do this for at least twenty minutes. It produces a very calm and clear mind, something essential for focusing and being in the flow of the market.

As a beginner you will find thoughts popping in and out of your mind faster than you can count. Do not fight them. Just see them float through as though you were watching clouds. Try to focus upon your breath by counting exhalations. I'll bet that you can't count up to ten breaths before becoming distracted. Eventually you'll get there. Do not become discouraged. Practice makes perfect. Just keep up your practice.

STEP TWO: VISUALIZATIONS

After I have prepared my mind, I try to visualize the many waves that occur during the trading day. There are up waves, and there are down waves. My job is to ride each wave as far as I can, no matter which direction. Basically I visualize a circle of prices moving in one direction or another. I see myself getting on that wave and, when it peaks or bottoms out, reversing and going with the next wave. I repeat this over and over again. I see myself taking losses quickly and also see myself riding winners for as long as possible. I try to do this for at least five minutes a day. Sometimes I repeat this routine at night before I go to bed. I believe it works because it cuts a neurological circuit that the brain is familiar with and thus can evoke quickly when needed. It is just my theory. All I know is that it works.

STEP THREE: AFFIRMATIONS

Affirmations are messages to your unconscious that help produce a given result. After I am done visualizing, I repeat over and over again the following silently to myself:

> *Every day and in every way I am able*
> *to let my profits run and cut my losses*
> *quickly. I am a winner.*

Basically, affirmations give you the opportunity to program your computer. In this case it is your subconscious.

What I have briefly outlined takes about thirty minutes. Like any other professional game player, you have to prepare yourself for your sport. In the trading game preparation is mostly mental.

STEP FOUR: EXTRAS

If I am in the trading pit and feel that I am losing it, I sometimes use the following techniques. I try to re-center myself by breathing slowly and deeply until I feel relaxed and focused again. A technique I learned in a workshop, called Open Focus® training, involves imagining spacial distances. This powerful tool produces a Samurai-like state of awareness that is perfect for the trading environment.

Chapter 14

HAIKU FOR TRADERS

Haiku for traders? Are you kidding? My whole purpose in reading and sometimes trying to create haiku poems is to get myself out of my thinking mode and into my feeling mode. I find that the contrast of the images in haiku poetry is beautiful, refreshing, and sometimes startling to the point of flashing insights into my inner person.

First, what is haiku poetry? In the original Japanese form, haiku consisted of alternate lines of five, seven, and five syllables in which the poet had to both convey a mood and present a picture that would challenge the reader's or listener's imagination. It was the shift in images using the most minimal of words that produced the pleasurable experience for the reader, the listener, and the poet. More often than not a direct or subtle reference to one of the changing seasons was a feature of haiku.

More macho readers should remember that many a Samurai warrior would create or read haiku before and after battle. I have sprinkled some of the most famous haiku throughout this book. Get a book of haiku poetry. I know that you will enjoy it. Take a haiku challenge and try to compose a few lines of verse. Enjoy!

Chapter 15

ZEN NOTIONS

And What Do You Think Is Your True Nature?

A snake wanted a ride across a pond and asked the turtle to give him a ride to the other shore. The turtle refused, saying that he didn't want to take a chance on the snake biting him. The snake pleaded and pleaded, saying that he wouldn't bite him. He promised over and over again that he wouldn't.

Finally, the turtle gave in and took the snake across the pond on his back. The snake got off, turned around, and bit the turtle. The turtle protested, "You promised not to bite."

The snake replied, "I can't help it. It's my nature."

Are you sure of your true nature despite all of your protestations to the contrary?

Mr. Dark Meets Mr. Sun

Darkness wondered what light looked like. Thus it came to pass that one day Mr. Dark said to himself, "I'll go visit Mr. Sun." So Mr. Dark left his home and traveled upward. As he approached Mr. Sun's home, the sky turned a golden color. As he arrived, he exclaimed to Mr. Sun, "This is wonderful. I have never experienced anything like this before."

After a while, Mr. Dark prepared to go home. Mr. Sun said, "I have never seen darkness, may I accompany you?" So Mr. Sun and Mr. Dark descended to earth and went deep into the darkest bowels of the earth. Mr. Sun looked around and said, "Well, where's the darkness?"

Everywhere Mr. Sun looked he did not see any darkness because. . . where there is light there can be no darkness.

Which Horse Are You?

Let's say that there are four kinds of horses: excellent ones, good ones, poor ones, and bad ones.

Before it sees the shadow of the whip the best horse runs slow and fast, left and right, at the jockey's will. Just before the whip touches its skin, the second best will run as well as the first one. The third one runs when it feels pain on its body. The fourth one will run only after the pain touches the marrow of its bones.

What does it take for you to become the first horse?

How Empty Is Your Cup?

A Zen master had a visitor who wanted to know more about Zen. Instead of listening, the visitor simply wanted to show off his own ideas as the master was pouring tea.

The master poured tea into the visitor's cup until it was full and then kept pouring.

Finally the visitor could not restrain himself. "Don't you see that my cup is full?" he asked. "You can't get any more in."

"You are right," said the master. And he stopped.

"And like this cup of tea, you are filled with your own ideas. How can you expect me to give you Zen unless you offer me an empty cup?"

Who Is Right?

One windy day two monks were arguing about a flapping banner across the shore.

The first said, "I say the banner is moving, not the wind."

The second said, "I say the wind is moving, not the banner."

A third monk passed by and said, "The wind is not moving. The banner is not moving. Your minds are moving."

Just Do It

A new monk came up to the master Joshu. "I have just entered the fellowship, and I am anxious to learn the first principle of Zen," he said. "Will you please tell it to me?"

Joshu said, "Have you already eaten your supper?"

The novice answered, "I have eaten."

Joshu said, "Now wash your bowl."

ZEN PARABLE

> *The direction we are facing has a lot to do with our destination.*
>
> THOUGHTS OF REV. SUNNAN KUBOSE

Suggested Readings

Journey of Awakening
by Ram Dass

•

The Open Focus Handbook
by Les Fehmi

•

The Inner Game of Tennis
by Tim Gallwey

•

The Centered Athlete
by Gay Hendricks and Jon Carlson

•

Suggested Readings

Zen in the Art of Archery
by Eugen Herrigel

•

The Ultimate Athlete
by George Leonard

•

Mastery
by George Leonard

•

How to Meditate
by Lawrence Le Shan

•

The Warrior Athlete
by Dan Millman

•

The Mental Athlete
by Kay Porter and Judy Foster

•

Fighting to Win
by David J. Rogers

•

Suggested Readings

Shambhala: The Sacred Path of the Warrior
by Chogyam Trungpa

•

You Gotta Want It
by Dick Woit with Steve Fiffer

•

Glossary

Ai
Harmony.

Bear
An opinionated person who believes that prices will fall.

Bear Market
A market in which the flow results in declining prices.

Breakout
A price gyration beyond the previous highs or lows.

Bull
An opinionated person who believes prices will rise.

Bull Market
A market in which the flow will result in rising prices.

Bushido
The conduct code for Samurai.

Call Option
A contract that gives the buyer the right to purchase the underlying commodity or security for a specified price in a specific time period.

Charts
A graphic depiction of previous price movement, worthless for determining future price determination.

Contrarian
A very opinionated person who goes against the flow of the market.

Day Trade
A trade that is offset that same day.

Enlightenment
The moment you know how little you really know.

Fundamental Analysis
Using economic data to forecast prices. (Traders refer to this as paralysis by analysis.)

Local

An exchange member or floor trader who trades for her/his own account.

Long

A position that benefits by rising prices.

Mushin

Pure consciousness of no thought.

Pit

The circular area on a trading floor where business is conducted.

Put Option

A contract that gives the buyer the right to sell a specific commodity or security at a given price for a specific period of time.

Resistance

The point at which rising prices stop.

Samurai

A warrior's warrior. A person who attacks his problem selflessly.

Satori
Pure enlightenment.

Sensei
A learned teacher.

Stop Order
A buy or sell order placed above or below the market that is executed when your predetermined price is hit.

Support
The point at which falling prices stop.

Switch Parameters
Those numbers that determine when the flow of the market has changed for you.

Tick
The minimum price fluctuation for a commodity or security.

Warrior
A person involved in resolving a conflict, be it internal or external.

Whipsaw
When price flow changes direction rapidly back and forth and back again.

Zen
Effortless effort. The religion of the Samurai.

The Warning

**Those who know
do not talk.
Those who talk
do not know.**

Samurai Trader's Maxim Number Six

FREE
SAMURAI TRADER'S
NEWSLETTER

SEND A SELF-ADDRESSED STAMPED
BUSINESS ENVELOPE TO:

SAMURAI TRADER'S
NEWSLETTER
SUITE 1120
30 S. WACKER DRIVE
CHICAGO, ILLINOIS 60606

Edward Allen Toppel can be reached by
e-mail via the Internet at
zentrader@delphi.com